## About the Author

He's a lovely man. He lives in Devon now. He's done a lot of things, like keep bees, design buildings and landscapes for sacred use, build the buildings too, have kids, lecture in fine art, watch birds endlessly, farm a smallholding, live in Osho's communes and in cities and in desert places on several continents, teach art as therapy, make furniture, write articles for international magazines, do nothing in a cave, exhibit his paintings, grow organic vegetables, have lots of grandchildren, write a book and get really into beekeeping.

The poems are the work of the last two years. The drawings are taken from the recent series *The Face Behind the Face*.

This is Rashid's third collection of poems and drawings. The first two books - *Life is one Blessed thing after another* and *Not Knowing guides our feet* - are both published by Tree Tongue and are available through the website.

This book and others available at
**www.treetongue.co.uk**

To my beloved Jordan
'nothing that we humans do
is ever right or wrong

# everything
## is
## something
## else

### rashid maxwell

Osho
ha
id

15
08
14

Published by Tree Tongue
22 Elm Road
Exmouth
Devon
EX8 2LG
www.treetongue.co.uk

ISBN 978-0-9546099-9-3

## Offering

these verbal sketches (poetry is such a crowded word)
are merely foot- and hand-holds cut into the snow face of my life
they also might provide assistance
to those I love and those who travel with me
and those of you I do not know journeying this way
they are not a sculpted staircase
but deliberate improvisations
for the cliff itself is ever-changing

so to all of you my children and grand-children
those I love friends and strangers
please accept this dedication
that is a tribute too
to the universe of Osho and the dawn of meditation

# Contents

# Driving Through Big Questions

Here's the thing about existence.
it's far too big for words.
even poetry whose lines
don't make it to the far side of the page.

Note how the windscreen wipers
counterpoint the bass drum on the radio
the grey brown landscape flashing past
counterpoints the bright blues of Van Gogh inside my head

This is it! Yet what does it mean?
love and hate, war in Mali, peace in Vietnam
bankers with too much, battery hens too little,
what do all these oppositions mean?

The car jinks left and holds a long curve right
driving through a sea of sky reflected.
I sat for thirteen years with Osho;
he left. I'm sitting with him still.

How do we find our way in life?
there is no way, he said.
the very idea of a way misguides
instead of going, think of coming

The car drives through a Van Gogh sea of windscreen wiper music
all the while the world goes flashing by.
nothing in existence has a meaning.
everything has – significance.

And what about who really is the driver?
who lives behind thes eyes and ears?
what about this consciousness that hasn't moved?

As I said it's far too big for words.

# Meditation Birthday

On my meditation birthday
we invite
the friends I most admire
to party

first at the door
is Joy
beside herself
already
bouncing off the walls
Patience brings a gluten-free
wheat-free non-dairy sugarless cake
then come the shy
the celebrated beauties
dark haired Silence and fair Stillness
Peace and Trust the newly weds
come hand in hand
ethereal and intimate
Truth (nee Verity) and Wisdom
have had a marital discordance
Compassion
taking photos with her mobile
has caught
Ecstasy
already out of his head
trying to get in someone's
- her name begins with S -
knickers
Silence faints clean away
while Wisdom never even
stops
to draw breath
let alone watch it

we have a high old time
in the end I herd
all of them
inside this book
and turn the page

# The Question

Who am I is
one of those
deft questions
that ricochet
carelessly to the heart of
everything
on the phone to my bank
at passport control
with small children or seated
quietly with roses

who am I

I must admit that I am one
who early on betrayed
his name and class
incorporated foolery
and the art of the wordless
took up neither being
nor not being
now the question who am I
floats void
and weightless

in the cool dawn air

le
20%
ent

## Credit card companies cut their limited appeal

The reason why cardholders with ex-cellent credit histories are seeing their limits cut is obvious (No credit where it's due, Money, 13 March). Cardhold-ers who religiously pay off the bill each month don't make any money (in terms of late interest payments) for the card companies: they don't want you. Credit card companies are in the busi-ness of making money (and right now they're desperate, especially if they're owned by a bank). Go and find another card, it's fairly easy. Companies don't seem to care about existing customers: they're hell bent on new customers.
**Allan Gould, Settle, North Yorkshire**

My card company cut my limit, with-out warning, to below what I owed, then charged me £12 for being over the new limit, though I did get a refund.
**smollett, guardian.co.uk/money**

I thought I was the only one when my limit was reduced from £3,000 to £500 by Nationwide last month, with a letter advising me of this I am sure I found offensive as I have never been in debt, and always pay my credit card bill promptly and in full.
**magical1, guardian.co.uk/money**

The lender is just deciding it doesn't want to give you as much of its money any more. It's under no obligation to do so (it might not have as much relative). Neither is it personal. And maybe it's a good idea to remind yourself you are a debtor, not a customer. Customers pay for stuff, they don't borrow money. The bank is doing you a favour. You are not doing it one in asking for more un-earned money. I find the entitlement of some people quite surprising really.
**oomph, guardian.co.uk/money**

Why is this a problem? If you have a good credit rating it is likely you can handle your finances and don't need a £15,000 limit. If you can't, you already have maxed out cards to add to your unsustainable mortgage.
**halo572, guardian.co.uk/money**

Here's a tip: have the money in the bank before you spend it.
**Adam Hayward, guardian.co.uk/money**

You always get those smug, patron-ising gits who bang on about putting money in the bank, and that they wouldn't be so feeble-minded as to have a credit card. Well try travelling around the world for work, hiring cars, booking into hotels, entertaining etc.
If you are human and can't file your expenses quickly enough, balances can rocket. In Paris a few weeks ago I tried to pay for a meal with my card, i knew to the pound what was on there. But the limit had been reduced without no-tice (apart from a letter I would collect on my return). It made me look a right mug as I scrambled for my debit card.

tailers. At some - dubbed "earn only" - you can't use reward money to reduce the cost of what you are buying and your balance will not appear on the card machine's receipt.
Here are some of the current deals: Until 15 May, spend £... or more at ... Express and get £5 reward money At Shell, between 1 April and 15 May, fill up five times with at least 5% of fuel, and earn 5% of the value of your ...visit.
...spend £25 or more at Yo! Sushi ...l and earn 5% off... ...ctricity to... ...get... toward... pay by Direct Debit and earn up to... more after a year (offer ends 17 May). You can't earn on "excluded... - gambling and lotteries, tobacco products, prescription medicines ... My money is on this being the reason behind their spoilt brat re-to... if we can do what we like under terms of the card".
..., guardian.co.uk/...

...quire more ...ulation!

...the New Forest it is impossible ...t) without an agent (Lettings ...ts' hidden hefty charges, Money, ...March). I am a mother on an ...ltural salary ... ...le to buy, and treated like ... landlords and agents. ...as to buy government ... ...o assist people like me - hard ...I have never taken benefits, but ...nable to afford housing. No council options; 5,000 people on the list and 70 properties come up each year. Why not have a government agency that helps over-rent direct to land-lords than the guarantee's they want, and offer valuable tenants like me some security. Moving has really affected my kids. I have paid some £80,000 in rent in the last nine years as to buy on my salary was impossible. Now I have to move again after a long tenancy. Goodbye deposit - land-lords don't accept wear and tear. No houses to rent in the bus area for my kids' schools; I am at work long hours; have to borrow £2,000 to move, etc. I feel absolutely desperate.
**maylbuye, guardian.co.uk/money**

I have a property which I let. I never use letting agents because I object to giving 15%-20% of my rental income for something I can almost do for free.

ting agreements, available online or in library books. Credit checks are a relatively small fee compared with the potential loss of unpaid rent. I never charge tenants a fee because the credit check is for my benefit, and it's unjus-tifiable for agents to charge a tenant for this.
I mention in the adverts that I am not a letting agent and will not charge tenants a fee. I can't stand letting agents. They find my ad online and contact me, offering to let my property, even though the ad always speci-fies no contact from agents. They are leeches, taking money from tenant and landlord for doing virtually noth-ing. As a profession it is inadequately regulated, with no requirement for any qualifications whatsoever. Anyone can set themselves up as an estate/letting agent. As long as landlords and tenants persist in using them, we are all throw-ing money down the drain.
**chunderboss, guardian.co.uk/money**

## Quote was Direct Line or losing my custom

I've just had my home insurance re-newal quote from Direct Line, which has followed a pattern for several years, in being ridiculously increased while undercut by its own website. Last year £298; quoted renewal (on Direct Line's website £264). In the past three years, when challenged, Direct Line has agreed to a price at or near the online quote. No... year; though a discount was greatly offered, the premium still increased by more than 50%. ...minutes on the web produced a range of better quotes for matching or improved cover, so Direct Line has lost my business. Apparently customer loyalty is seen as not merely valueless but a chance for opportunist profit. ...that for every person like me, there will be many more who don't re... or challenge their automatic re...al. Loyalty isn't appreciated and perhaps naively, I find that very sad.
**Ian Helm, Oldham**

## The ... interest rate conundrum of Isas

Your recent articles on Isas have been very interesting but they all raise the question of why banks pay lower rates of interest these than on other saving accounts. You would think Isas would be cheaper to run than other accounts since the banks don't have to go to the trouble of deducting income tax and paying it to HMRC. Surely the banks couldn't be nicking some of our tax relief, could they? I doubt it was the government's intention when creating Isas that banks should cream off half the customers' benefits.
**Martin Parker, Bookham, Surrey**

Write to Your Shout, Guardian Money.

# OMG this Autumn
for Joshua

OMG this autumn
        day won't come again
the driven light the green
        leaf sloping into death
are now and nevermore.

photographs don't do it
        the river needs a new
name every second every
        inch. Its sound and shape
are now and nevermore.

the candle flaming up
        is always different flames
who knows perhaps the whole
        point of this life is always
now and now and now

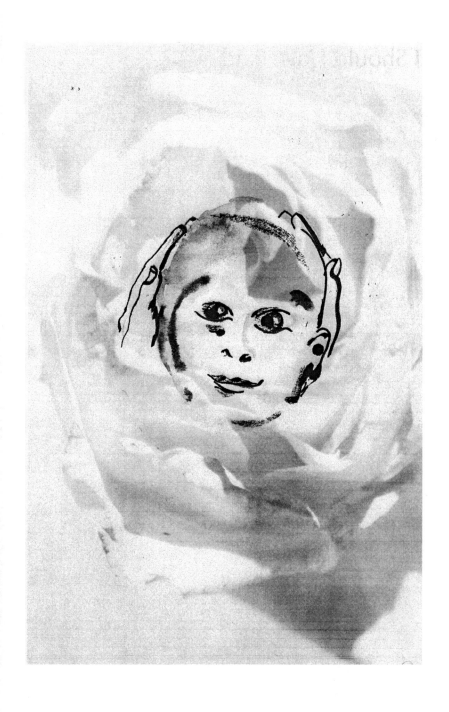

# d Have Said

I should have said
when you were bending over me
lassoing me with mala and a new name
nearly forty years ago
I should have told you that
I would be the ground you walked on
and the bed you slept on
the air you moved in and
your body moving in it
I would have liked to be the shower
that cools you twice a day
the chai you drink
your right hand and
your knitted hat

no matter I said nothing then
in realms beyond the mind
time ceases to exist
I say now it is all
already happening

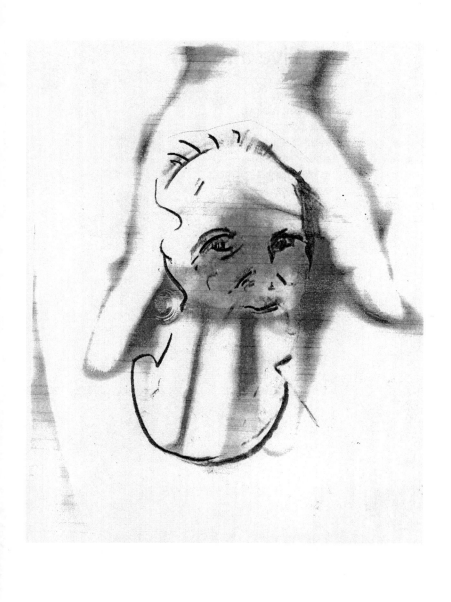

# At Five a m

At five am
i am amphibious
sink slowly
in a hideous ooze
slowly rise
in blue forget-me-nots
wakefully
i circumvent the nets
of this marauding
dreamed-up mind
ubiquitous I am
at five am

# Mister Fox

today at dawn
my totem Mister Fox
moves along the hedgerow
scribbles long tail secrets in the snow
queries scents
deciphers sounds

for years i sat at Osho's feet
breathing in pure air
here today i stumble
in the cloudy
confines of
a tiny mind

walk through a wood or open moor
a movement
gone before you see it yet
you know
you know it was a mistle thrush
that knowing!

where is wholeness
that I know yet do not know?
where light i glimpse yet do not see?
where is the truth
transient as Mister Fox
that flashes in these words?

# Sometimes I Just Sit

sometimes
i sit there
and think
sometimes
i just sit he says
rain comes
putters on uncountable
leaves the neighbour feeds
her horses from a
clanking bucket

now I walk out
in the lanes
careful not
to bring
words along
hills and grass-
green valleys
up and fly
into the faded purple
protective is the sky

verges and hedgerows
soft buffers
our genial guide
all things are for
this suspended
glory moment only
we have to take down
our verbal selves
to see that grace
is scattering the way

Beloveds
people of an ever faster
turning world
pause today
exactly on the threshold
of real treasure
and real trouble

You two – Sam and Jordan
have known life
under open skies
felt storms and starlight
have been enclosed
in buildings clothes
ideas beliefs

You two – my Beloveds
know the pleasures and the perils
of enclosure
the open sky above
reminds you of the open sky within
all skies both grey and blue
are daily birthday gifts to you

# Love's Reminder

The wave of love curves over us
forever
as in the Hokusai print
waits to wash away
already failing do-it-yourself selves
we live
in lark song and sheet lightening
an exaltation of fan vaulting and blasted quarries
bright meadows and the blade that ploughs them
the deep shade of a watchful wood

love wants to sweep away fear
remind us that we come from love
are made of love
that love is the core and cover of things

# the Fox Said

In the woods a fox
looked down my seventy third year

on your birthday you lost your credit cards
and driving licence in the Paris metro.
a radiant lady, laughing, took you to a bank
the labyrinth at Chartres was opened for you.
       that is one leg called Gratitude.

you photographed the coldest christmas anyone remembers.
a pipe burst in your garage
a steady man, laughing, told you
cut it, roll it and hammer it.
       that is another leg called Trust

in the spring you worried time was running out
for all the drawing, beekeeping, writing
and building your new greenhouse.
your beloved, laughing, sat you down and kissed you.
       that is a third leg called Love

when summer came you said the streetlight
by your house should be removed
the neighbours gathered round with poisoned spears
this tart event helped you to find your measure.
       that leg is called Dignity


the fox said
with four legs you are fit
to find the heaven hidden here on earth.
the earth draws you down from the lover's moon
the earth draws you down from the starry way
the earth draws you down from the passionate sun
the earth draws you down from the infinite blue

everything is here
everywhere is here.

# Looking back

looking back
it seems
this life began
when Osho smiled at me behind his folded hands
some thirty years ago

the former life lives on brilliant
in the sons and daughters
the scattered seeds of destiny

i am stamped with blue skies and the warm nights of Poona
with crimson hibiscus and orange lilies
in the green tropic of the ashram

with being first in line for discourse
with swimming in the master's eyes
working my ass off in the veggie garden
with dissolving in the silence of ten thousand intimates

we learned to fly a sunken submarine
when he died we sang awash
with tears of gratitude
as flames consumed his flesh

now the friends
daring in their trust
are scattered
the dangerous bloom of lovingness gives out
its fragrance everywhere.

we don't look back as a rule,
he's in our every molecule

# Surrender

Clamorous quiet provokes offence
or retreat behind fortified walls

Yet silence is only the vanguard
sent to recapture this castle from outlandish ego

Freedom advances slowly mopping up resistance
one by one the tower and redoubts are reclaimed

The Queen arrives unannounced
surrender is unpreventable now

Her reign is generous
Her laws are Love and Life and Laughter

This is the real
State of Grace

13

# A Poem for Devon in Spring

## Part I

Buttercup Samphire Squirrel-tail Saxifrage
Dandelion Deadnettle Dropwort Furze
Oxeye Daisy Suffocated Clover
Eyebright Fleabane Purslane Spurge

Bulrush Burdock Mollyblobs Hyacinth
Waterwhorl Woundwort Woodruff Thrift
Stinking Hellebore One-flowered-wintergreen
Kingcup Kidney Vetch Bryony Broom

Honeysuckle Horse Mint Weasel-snout Scabious
Speedwell Fescue Foxtail Thyme
Purple Loosestrife Thin-runner Willowherb
Fat Hen Forget-me-not Feverfew Flax

## Part II

Hollocombe Putford Punchardon Petrockstow
Honeychurch Holsworthy Huntsham Huish
Bratton Clovelly Broadwoodkelly
Lapford Landkey Winkleigh Ash

Hazelbury Hoxton Sixpenny-Handley
Luffincott Satterleigh Lundy Lee
Challacombe Common Cheriton Ridge
Dolton Dowland Cheldon Croyde

Exeter Exwick East Down Eggesford
Holdsworthy Hatherleigh Three-Hammer Hill
Zeal Monochorum Barton-in-the-Willow
Chudleigh Chulmleigh Chawleigh Week

# Bird-watching with Grace

In the muffled tree bent over a river
- some sort of fig I think -
I saw the secret or the token

the journey there is arduous
slippery underfoot fast flowing water
sharp rocks greedy crevasses

Grace comes with me
mysterious joyous intimate
when I roll up my trousers

remove my shoes
she gathers up her skirt with elegance
steps into the translucence

we make it to an island
cross a sandy cove with strange engravings
cross a silk lagoon

one more crossing where the river rushes
there's my place
a throne of rock beside white-water rapids

now starts the waiting and the watching
Grace is silent
a dark hawk watches from a high dead branch

pale clouds and the rocks
the water and the trees
assume a gentle dance outside of time

Grace points
and from the stooped old fig
an iridescent bird loops out turquoise blue and black

through my binoculars I see it has a crimson eye
I am in love. Irena Puella – Fairy Bluebird
gravity is gone

Grace lifts us high into the dance
unmoving dance
outside of time

# Self Portrait of the Artist

In the woods
now the springtime of autumnal fruit
the artist listens to
the scratch
of twigs on twigs
sees the to and fro
of form and space
all things bloom
when they are honoured
the artist is
the ever present subject of his art
he has amassed a layered lamina
of who he is
now is the time
to scrape the layer of ochre and alizarin
unpaint the false
the trees
reach down
to offer their translucence
please forgive the artist
as another film of colour
ripples and compresses
on the palette knife
he has thinned
the picture
into this pale wash of warm sienna
one day
his portrait will arrive
at proper likeness
clear white
canvass

# What on Earth

When danger looms
sheep huddle in a flock
we human sheep expect
the worst.
now is the time to take stock of
our trampled habitat
and restless crushing impetus
the looming precipice.

This era is of human rights
the valued individual
we have evolved to be ourselves
and part of all that is
as we are born alone we die alone
it's time to say goodbye to Teddy Bear deities
and puppet priests corrupted politicians
big businesses that gobble up our lives.

It's time to find the meaning of creative
loving
beautiful courageous conscious free
intelligent - awake to our truth.
when is the day of our human return
let's switch off the smartphone
step out of the herd
sing dance and laugh

let's step out on the journey into
what on earth?

NOT WHO
WE THINK

# Love and Meditation Can

Forty years
from now
there'll be no trade
or shops

3D printers and
the new
nano-technology
will print out
all you need

hell is the pull of gravity
our brutish past of fear
and blind desire
a life without
awareness.

the wise ones say
that only love and meditation
give you eyes
grace is falling upwards
to the heavens
better than a ten thousand and one D printer
any day

# Thankful to be Thankful

When sun erupts
from slate dark
autumn skies I thank
my lucky stars for Osho
he spread his wholeness
so that everything I am
is his

thank god he brings today
a sunrise to my sunset
silk planes of water
to my tea-cup storms
points out to me safe routes
through quaking mires of every
day

I'm thankful he's the poet
of my wordless longing
the magic man
who turns into the one
who massages each night
these raw and restless
feet

he is the cool breeze
from the east
and he who holds my face
into the warm west wind
he tells me when
to shut my mouth and
drink

a master is
the shelter from
the downpour of desire
the scorching heat of shame
he long out-lives his body
in my grateful
heart

beloved of my
heart of hearts you
open up the pure land
for our skilful
occupation
I am thankful to be thankful

# Knock knock
for Sofiia

knock knock
on the pearly gates
St Peter says who's there?
boo.
boo who?
don't cry. it's only a joke.

who's there?
who am i?
who are we?

this right hand rests
like ripe fruit on the key
board. am i in this hand
its platelets and its chromo
somes? or possibly
i'm in the heart that loves
and lurches clots and stops?

what if i am not the
who i think? In this
body? more like a no
body who witnesses
the comings and the goings
of what I call myself?

knock knock
who's there?
you
you who?
yahoo! I told you
it's only a joke

# Twenty Past Nine

matter it seems
does not exist
only energy is
the real is really invisible
beyond both
birth and death
our life is
a counterfeit life

twenty past nine
on the eve of mine
light rain has turned
to disorderly snow
i plan my days
on what i know
the unknown
is what shapes them

# I am an ing

I am an ing
a common or garden possible ing
sitting and thinking
shifting and drinking
singing and loving and seeding and weeding
ing-ing away the whole fucking day

Living is happening
everything's changing
everything's always ing-ing
being and doing and toing and froing
loving and crying breathing and dying
stopping is ceasing to be an ing

I am an ing a potential ing
at the very very beginning
feeling and knowing
and growing and healing
to come to the clear understanding
that there's nothing at all beyond the wall
but a ringing
                unending
                        ing-ing

# Haiku

In the shopping mall
everything's available
but not sun and fresh air


The motor cyclist
guns his yellow motor bike
a pink rose shivers


Shedding its old bark
the Red Eucalyptus tree
like a sannyasin.


All these wealthy homes
only the big garage doors
are smiling


Excellent coffee
excellent view of the car park
Life is thorns and roses

11
01
13

# What Have we Done!

(On New Year's Day)

This black hole night engulfs the cries of sufferers;
of rape in Delhi and kids massacred at Sandy Hook,
of bombings in Damascus, murders in Peshwar,
assassination in Accra, child abuse in London.
The corpses are all swept away, their cries devoured.
This is our precious world rashid. Say what can be done?

On radio the presidential body-guard
tells how he threw himself across the limo's back seat
covering the Kennedys. He saw the brainless broken skull.
Jackie cradled close the body, crying out,
What have they done? What have they done? The body-guard
became, for thirty years, a lonely alcoholic.

I read a history of the First World War. Blind
generals , my grandfather among them,
order numberless battalions into a no-mans-land of bullets.
Country boys and college graduates climb rotting mounds
of bodies into fields of brother ghosts and screaming shells
till they themselves are torn apart. What have we done?

The sun and moon shine down upon the tyrant and the victim,
the rapist and the huddled corpse. My heart is shuddered open
by our shamelessness. Humanity! What have we done!
Yet soon the first slow light of dawn appears. The mind falls quiet.
All this is seen as happenstance. Not wrong. Not right.
Love arousing Consciousness.

# A Man I Met

a man i met
who wasn't there
told me that enlightenment
(or put more simply god)
was what transcends particulars
particles? i said i'm slightly deaf
if you like, he said
yet god lives only in particulars
he followed on
this is our living paradox
paradise? i said
if you like he said.

# Sannyas is a Love Affair

Beloved one your call invited
me to move into your home perched
high up on the cliff above the sea of stillness
i said i wasn't ready yet.

you told me i could be a god like krishna
the lover of all women
i went on hanging out with
flashers at the winkleigh bus stop

you said 'i will love you for ever'
i went bright red and
turned away worried
what the neighbours might be thinking

you held me in your arms offered
me the freedom
of your spacious estates
i said i'd stay behind bars a while longer

compassion made you gesture
i couldn't dodge your stick
knocked me conscious
of unconsciousness

now the love affair is consummated
you've disappeared inside my skin along
with all the sunlight and the birdsong
laughing at my fumbled jokes

# Only One Moment

This moment
in the sunlit
garden with
the willow warbler
and the step
that needs
repair
the crumpled
crowing
of the rooster
this moment
with the
looping foxglove
swallowed
by the moment
following
a pencil
scratting
in the dusty
shed's
bright slanting
beams
by moments
at the cobbled
keyboard
and now
words fading
gracefully into
the silence
of another now

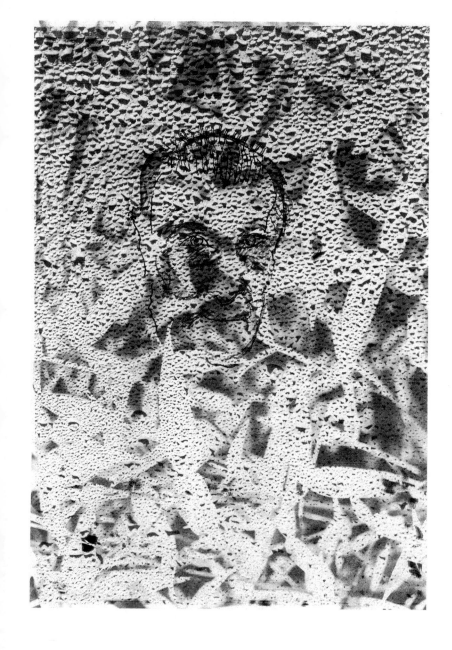

# Transmission

Across the faded London square
a crow calls on and on
I walk with three who honour both the worlds
transmit the mysteries
the inner to the outer

In a great museum's
oriental gallery
we stand before a statue
that was itself conceived
to transmit consciousness

We are a line of suitors
waiting for the glance of grace
the sandstone body is eroded
by the constant current
of reflective eyes

Crowds flow to either side of us
their chatter and their clatter are waves breaking
on a distant shore
the buddha speaks precisely slowly
with his full lips and his silence

The tide recedes
the sand is smoothly washed
the god reveals a sheen
of purest possibility

A crow calls in the square outside.

# Splitting Oak Logs
For Noa and Inigo

The unity of things

An oak tree cracked and laid down in the gale a few weeks back.
Grandsons, sons and I cut it carefully to lengths for cleaving.

Splitting logs is worship, is a bonded labour of love
and it shows us the delicate wiring of bodies and minds

Too big to lift – I trundle a bole downhill
And up a ramp of small logs to the chopping block.
Okay now! Here's how to split it.
Face the bole squarely, knees slightly bent.
Hold the axe with both hands, horizontal across the body.
The eyes are softly focussed on the place you want the axe to strike.
You are a swordsman warrior awaiting the foe;
An artist waiting for the thunderbolt that opens up the canvass.

Destruction and creation

When the body and the mind are still,
the right hand hefts the axe-head high,
The left hand follows it aloft,
the right hand slides down toward the left
the axe gives way to gravity.
The body bows forward, pulls down the axe.
The blade delves through the widening rings.

With a moist thunk the log rives open
along the line of most submission.
Two pale membranes open up a distant memory.
Their sweet-sour smell awakens you
to endless lives lived on this earth.

Gratitude like love.

You bow to the still presence of trees and woods
to the net of rooks poised in the evening sky.
Now you bow to the circle of sun and rain,
and bow to the mind that accords and decrees.
And you bow to the body that you became;
the flesh that bridges desire and delight
that hews and heaves and talks and smells,
seeks light like a tree and will still be felled.

# Karva Chauth

In parts of India women fast from sunrise to moonrise for the safety and
longevity of their man

Grace says that when you deeply love someone
you want to give your age to them

When someone offers you their age
there is an urge to clear the debris of your life
the shame of failed affairs
and failing sight and broken hopes
your pride and arrogance the fear of disillusion
death and dullness

In a gallery in Amsterdam
I saw a painting of a white haired man in prison
they are starving him
a young girl stands before his cell - through the bars she offers him
her radiance
her creamy breast from which he drinks

Clear the stale to make way
for the radiance of grace
fall down giddy with a strain of adolescent love
spend long days sitting in the corrugated
hills be the ocean's overture
flush yourself of who you aren't

# Between two Worlds

oh friends
we find ourselves
between two worlds
in the sheer jewels of the bathroom shower
or stalled at traffic lights heart attuning
to the slow beat of the wipers
and randomly at births and funerals
somewhere between departure
and arrival we are not
where we thought

the ancient world was innocent
we mated freely
sliding in behind the women
bathing in the river
we maimed the men who came
to oust us from
our bounded ground
our instincts kept us innocent
look we have conquered the whole world now
that old world is within us still

over the water is
the poised tranquillity we aspire to
dawn spreads across pale vapour fields
mountains with their crest in cloud
woods that sparkle after gentle rain
mysterious until awareness
the great sun rising
dissolves our separate instincts
until we know we are the breath and breadth
of everything

# Waiting without Waiting

In meditation
everything is something else

meditation is called waiting without waiting
silence is another word for all that is
sunrise is a name for heart in labour
the glimpse of a tidal bore is smile
death translates as natural neighbour
solar system means a blade of grass
peace is a vacant room - an understanding – war
the first act of your day is called beloved
thank you is your secret name
the song of any bird is something

Meditation is a waiting without waiting
waiting for no thing
when nothing arrives
as a thirty metre wall of emptiness
who is there to meet it
or to wait
or meditate?

## ...ie Moon Said

last night full moon occurred at three twenty five

i dressed and stood in the garden
of gleaming grey roses cool air
the moon said look and listen rashid
so i did

a belt of cloud bisected the sky
silence echoed round the bowl of the world
the moon said keep standing in let-go and silence
so I did

let love break the boundaries of self it said
be free of time and space
let all ideas disintegrate all beliefs dissipate
till there's only the seeing left
so I did

the seeing
that nothing exists but the seeing
nothing-but-seeing sees every thing
osho and bashar assad einstein picasso
pol pot and bosnian thugs those who are tortured
and those who torture

mountains mists tigers ticks
whales krill planets atoms
the beautiful brutal caboodle
of life and death in the universe
is nothing but seeing
that consciousness sees

see said the moon that seeing is all
and I did

# Water Regularly

These frail green salad leaves
and pallid roots
faint in my brutish hands
how can they live
how dangerous  it is to press
them into cold brown ground

earth graded turned
raked even
wormed with compost
still I doubt the soil will
take to such profound a frailty

all anyone can do
is trust that life loves life
that
and water regularly

# Another Day     at Home

One star
blinded by the slow grey
dawn from bed
I look inside for who
I was was blown apart
by scattered dreams today
the guy I re-assemble is
well colourful authentic
built to last but prone
to wear and tear I draw
a cloak of skin around him
outside three young oaks
begin to glow like orange
lances stood against
the damson mottled northern
sky a nuthatch works
the mossy deadwood I
allocate the coming hours
and minutes writing cooking
cutting out the brambles
now starts another day
at home

Look
in our hearts there is
a city graced with spires
and minarets and shopping
malls and classy brothels
the city's in a continent
of forests fields and deserts
the continent is in
a world of festivals
and wars the world is in
a universe of gasses
bursting into supernova
on and on and on
who sees all this who
manages and nourishes
imagines and forgets
this unimaginable and
unforgettable existence it is
you your formless consciousness
the real you
try this
at home

# A Tick in the      Health Food Shop

a stranger
in the health food shop
accosted me between
the split peas and the wholegrain
malted loaves she said
weren't you on the telly
last night was it you
discussing fatherhood
the blood-gorged tick of ego
is a parasite of truth
I simpered manfully
in simulated self
effacement oh not that
old programme run again
this year I have a show
of etchings and my book
is coming out and then
inside I cursed myself
this old rapacious bloated
ego

a baby
by the exit held me
with his eyes giant cosmic
telescopes to probe
the dark beyond I leaned
into the buggy fell
ten thousand thousand light
years into lovingness
I lived for twelve years with
a master he was in there
laughing to remind me
that the ego is a hand
me down bewitchment
a fiction neither curse
nor blessing and you suffer
when you want things other
than the way they are
love said your ego needs
a fattening up before
it drops

# A Tale                    of Marmalade

Mrs Baveridge
my great aunt's cook made forceful
marmalade I have
her recipe the secret
is to almost burn
the bitter Seville oranges
with unrefined brown sugar
when the jam is due to set
I'm bothered and high pitched
stoke the fire with sparky
willow logs and test
the mixture frequently
the house smells thickly of
some grove in Andalucia
when the sweating's done
the jars gleam darkly rows
of walnut coloured
memories

Mr Shakespeare
said the world's a stage
I play the cook and poet
you the reader and
the judge we're nothing special
two of half a dozen
thousand million figments
of the cosmic energy
sparks in darkness blazing
for a moment life
condenses into matter
then expands back into
energy our death
is not a death at all
oranges aren't ultimate
results and marmalade
is fundamental energy
in transit

# Bickering    at Tiverton

A dark
form lifted on my right
the car was overheated
we'd started bickering
at Tiverton
I thought it was a pigeon knew
it couldn't be
I braked what's happening
she said the bird flew up
and over us now her side
keeping pace
the short neck and the pointed
slate-grey plunderous wings
a Peregrine we said
suddenly the air
seemed sweet the moor
a holy place it tipped
a wing and slipped a fading feral
freedom on the sodden
ochre moor

Unscrew
your head reach in remove
with care the quibbling
mind
ah silence
tingles for a while holds
emptiness and everything
both truth and things imagined
holiness and horror
it's possible to find
peace and actual freedom
re-learn what children know
the sweetness in this torn
and troubled world
to glide untroubled
as a falcon
breasting waves of winter
forever free of north
and south forever free of
bickering mind

# The Circle of our Days

Leaves of
beech and maple linger
as the last upholders
of the foxing light
I pull the haulms of beans
and lift the yellow late
potatoes fork the gleaming
soil lay humus on
the broken beds rooks
scatter in their rookery
chatter of the coming night
the pitch dark beds once
frenzied with ripe fruit
and emerald leaves are now
inert turned in upon
themselves collapsing into
nullity I lean against the mossy
garden gate the dying
day hangs darkly on
the valley.

The waste
these aches and pains of age
the loss of innocence
missed trains botched jobs the curse
of choosing comfort over
consciousness not letting
happen that which had
to happen shame heaps up
through the years now resting
on the damp green gate
I see the ordered beds
and watch the rufous clouds
slide low across mid Devon
I see at last there is
no waste whatever happens
makes the compost for
another life we leap
from humus into bright
humanity then crumble
back to earth

# The Fog      that Reveals

Fog
hung thick and raindrops
beaded on the branches
in the valley of our youth
we loved the horror and
the hanky-panky snorted
with the monsters
close to hand the rotten
school teachers strict priests
and men with clipped moustaches
who terrorise the spirit
sometimes we heard a lonely
flute a fighter plane
a nightingale or crying
a wise man beckoned us
poured us wine of his own vintage
we sipped it and the fog
began to lift we saw
our valley was a ruined
paradise

One
more glass and I was smashed
he poured another one
I don't remember anything
he stole my coloured pencils
the layout of our future
now we don't have much
to cling to we can travel
light as we arrived
pain comes and goes
grief
comes and goes yet we
are walking in a field
that has no gravity
a fullness that has nothing
i'm trying to say that freedom
in this life is possible
I'm trying to say that sunlight
fills the land the fog is in
the mind

# The Goddess

                    i've
waited for you for
some time can't remember
if it's hours or eons
i glimpsed you recently
in chartres cathedral lady
chapel and another
time in bed at dawn
in order to entice you
I will paint you or
empoem you bring
you back to daily life
where you belong
are you blonde or dark
norse or pre-hellenic
i visualise your skin
your lips the luminous
cascade of hair sweet lady
are you wrathful or
maternal how should i
address you

# I Just Realised

                    silly
questions how can i
not be addressing you
oh my boundless love
i see you with my eyes
wide shut i touch you
in the empty air
you're out beyond the senses
like climbing up a hill
and at the top keep climbing
i thought you were remote
clothed in beauty truth
and consciousness yet all
these rainbow flowers acidic
seas and rivers warring
politicians grieving
kids and snoring neighbours
how can they not be
your face you take my words
away and leave me only
these

# The Size      of Life

A poem
needs a form to hold
the fleeting words perhaps
a Devon longhouse settled
in the land white walls
old flagstone floors
four up four down and at
the heart a steady burning
stove a fridge well stocked
the cheeses on the top
shelf bottles in the door
and vegetables in plastic
drawers the living of
the house is in the loving
and the fighting and
the fucking and the eating
life billows through the walls
the garden and the land
Afghanistan and Mars
way beyond our
lives

So quiet
the house tonight a tap's
slow drip the pendulum
of this old heart a north
wind soothing on the window
pane the silence lifts me
on its billows through
the walls and out beyond
the limits of the limitless
neutrinos travel faster
than the speed of light
silence too is high
velocity no form
or payload bodiless
yet still a tap's slow drip
a soothing of the wind
the drumming of a trusty
heart pervades in every
corner of the universe.
beyond our little
lives

# Real Poetry

Real poetry
is not this leap
from ear and eye
to brain
to heart
nor the metaphor
of autumn sunlight
brilliant on an apple green
hay field beneath
a towering
blackberry cloud
and
and not the rhyming or
alliteration
of our daily flukes and synchronicities
no
real poetry
is wordless

this ringing silence


this




                    this

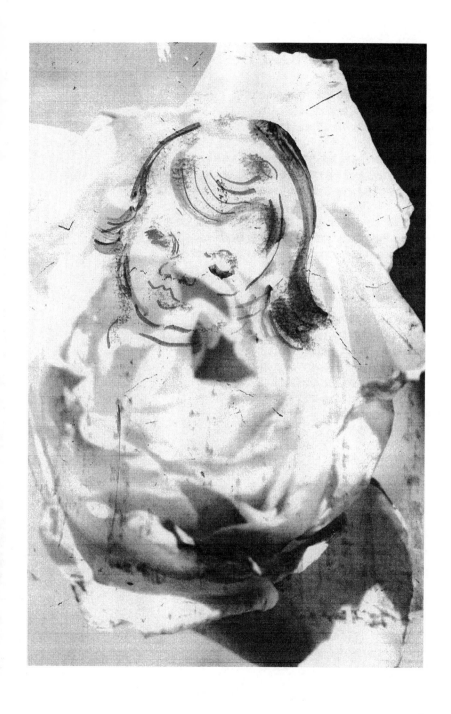

# Passengers not Pilots

Should we build our house here
across from the patient forest
on the river's broad meander?

Or maybe here where the sea laps carelessly
and crows and egrets web the water
this place where merchants trade their perfumed sacks?

Should we maybe build here in this zodiac
when the earth transits towards Aquarius
turns from old complacency to new concern?

We could be happy.

Yet we are passengers not pilots
on this flying trip
our true home is elsewhere.

A master points us to our long time home
our long forgotten birthright
this palace hidden
deep within the lost land of ourselves.

Here.

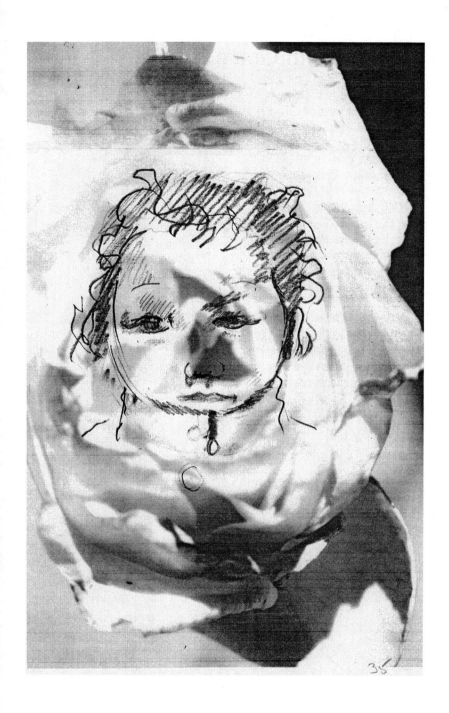

35

# Meeting with Grace

make a bonfire of words
when the moment of meeting arrives.
start a small heap with
'and' and 'the' and 'in' and 'but'
and 'no' and 'god' and 'if'.
set the brilliant orange flames

climbing high through the hoard;
then pile on middle-weight words
'ourselves,' 'possession.' 'restraint,'
'service,' 'orgasmic,' ,forever.'
when the flames unsay the words
throw on the heavy, holy ones;

'consciousness,' 'cosmic,' 'eternal.'
let them burn in the lapping tongues
we watch side by side the crimson
dance till the dark night falls and
reinvents the silent magic
of not two.

# Answering your Question

The dark earth
soft as love
presents its breast
I kneel before it
transplant
lettuce seedlings
delicate butterflies
in the hand
arrange the
scattered patterns
into shallow hollows
in weeks they are
a brief feast
life's span
is seen as swift and
full of grace
that's what
the master
Osho showed us
generosity
this fruitful
beauty

# Rain Steps Quietly

(for Sofia and Ciara)

Rain steps
quietly
a cat
on dry leaves
the pre-dawn
rattle
of the rooks
the night so pitch
a chance
to flood this form
with birdsong
and the damp
must of the
woods
be stuffed
with night's
dark nothingness
what comes to form
returns to formlessness
the quiet black cat
moves on
a cockerel convenes
the light
these wear-worn
words queue
up to bless
the rising
day

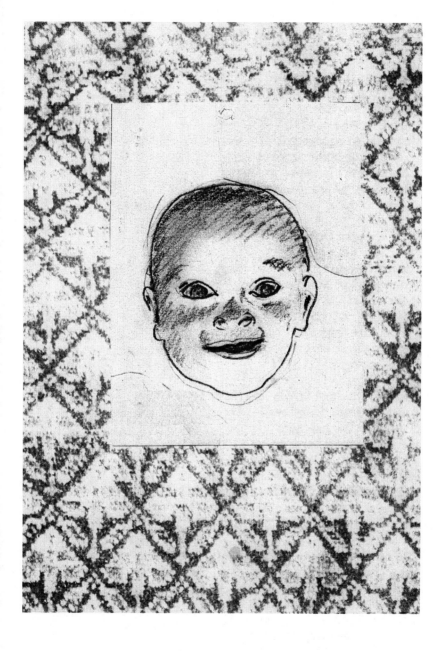

# On the Crowded Train

Somewhere between exeter
and london i look out
the train is thundering a ton
you are looking in
clothed in emerald meadows
yellow button buttercups and
apple blossoms blooming in your hair
i ride your smile from tiverton
       to delhi

In the speeding train
i hear your heels approach
i do not have to turn my head
i know you'll sit with me
in the new religion-less religion
grace is the only goddess
i watch your fingers ball
the food that feeds my
       being

Businessmen shout fiercely into mobiles
dump the greek derivatives
close down our exposure
the night express bores on
i'm old enough to know
what these men think insoluble
that grace can rise in any place
and set all obstacles
       to rest

Our hearts are quiet
the rocking train slides past
a distant hill where caves conceal
a grey wind-horse called grace
grace carries us across a copper sky
from where all things are bright
nothing that we humans do is either wrong or right
everything in truth is
       you

39

# Love's Word

bluebell sky
sways the hammock
oaks high-rise
in raven's raucous tract
not less loving
than the soothing dove's

this word love
contains
huge spaces and
an intimate closeness
the smile of sunrise at midsummer
and the frigid winter solstice

your love
moves with the breeze
across my skin
is always
always here

love's not the words
but the space in which
they ricochet and resonate
in which
the oak the sky and the raven
flare and grow silent

# To Light a Thousand Suns

I can't do that anymore -
throw out the days half-eaten
this body has to die one day

monsters made of steel and glass
suck in their prey at nine o'clock
spit the skins out half past five

oak trees make a million acorns
bees make surplus honey
earth itself is pure abundance

look inside — we are not slaves
we have within ourselves
the spark the seed the strike
let's call it spirit soul or life
enough to light a thousand suns

# Devotion

Beside the bonfire
lies a plastic doll
melted
to resume its formless origin
just so
sitting in the cool fire
of your beauty
there is fusion
may I stay here?

# Oh Dear

Oh dear
this poem
is again the same
as the last one
and the ones before
always saying
to the youniverse
thank you
thank you
thank you
for this
unerring heartbeat
and the treasury
of brilliance held
behind these locked-down lids
for buckled ears
that funnel in
an orchestra of sound
and for a mouth
of ripe crushed tastes
for a life
that blazes briefly
as a comet
as grace
and thank you
for a mind
to finely frame
these silly words
thank you
my dear

# This Pilgrimage
(for Ciara)

In the red bus
to the concert
asking everyone
where to disembark
i figured
there are sixty years between us
someone pointed
with their gps
next stop

your grand
grand-daughter hand
in mine i wished
this jig-mazed pilgrimage
through shiny kensal rise
would carry on
forever

the singer
with her rainbow saree
and bright filigree tamboor
rose from a deep well
of silence
took us
circling the whale-dark
urban sky

I saw you
give yourself
to love of sound
and weightlessness
I saw it's taken
sixty years
to see this pilgrimage
goes on and on
forever

# In Spain

In Spain there is
a valley
barren and remote
where once a year
ground water rises
waist high
thick as bollards
from the ground

The Master works
for many years
with digging bar and feather
on our granite plates
love is his purpose
and his product
pouring down
the valleys of the world

His love wells up
in meditation
unfathomable
starts the slow
engulfment our
fragile sandstone forts
is pouring down
the valleys of the world

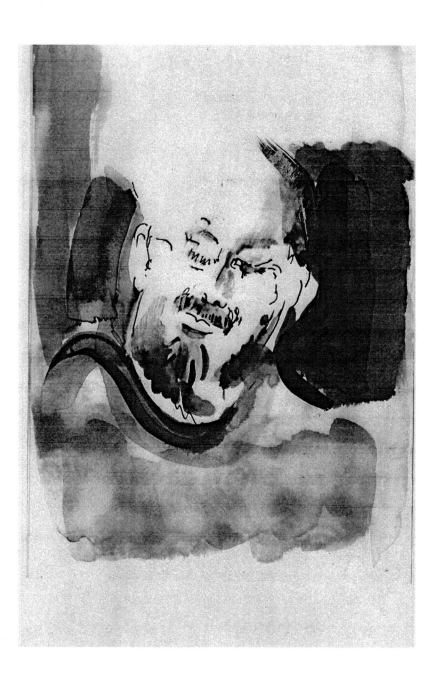

# Don't Worry be Happy

The arrow is unerring
the river finds it's
random course
this tumbling life
has no intent
other than to live itself
don't worry be happy
the bitter break-up
and the brilliant break-through
the tyrant's birth
the infant's howling death
are one event

you want to worry
be unhappy
good that too is life's
secret whisper of love
the more you rise
in love's transparency
the more you see
that you are me
that we are everyman
and every thing
love knows
no good and bad

the bitter plum
is sister to
the soft implosion
of the crimson strawberry
love lives as hitler
and as krishna
fukushima and
mount etna
all are love's ritual display
don't worry
be happy
the arrow is unerring

# Another Word for Poetry

Small nubs of summer wait
in buds of winter twigs

everyone can be a poet
call up sunlight
sifting through a wood
or conjure seaweed swaying in
the pale green waves

poetry submerses us
in worlds bigger than the world

staring once in dappled forest light
part of it detached
a leopard moved away
she had been looking at us all along

loves's another word for poetry
what we look for and look with

not only that
it's looking at us all along.

# Know Yourself

The bedroom window is half open

an immense invisible python
steals through the doubtful night
a thousand thousand autumn leaves
shiver in the east wind
scatter on their everlasting flight

sit cross-legged on the bed

there's no such thing as a thing
says quantum physics
sub-atomic particles exist as pure potential

a deep self rises from the scattered
molecules of body
rests itself in the void

know yourself as this

# Jesus Passing By

Jesus passing by
knocked on our door
I was somewhat surprised
Jesus I said come in
come in for a cuppa tea
tea? have you got no wine?
okay so give me water I will make my own
what's all this son of god stuff? I asked
oh that he replied that was my way of saying
all things are a piece of something else
all things are actually a part of
consciousness
what they used to call god
and Paul got it totally wrong
we are all sons of god including
this non-biodegradable teabag
and he tossed it in the landfill bin
oh okay I said - like the Buddhist thing
yeah I got it from his guys in India
Christ Almighty I ejaculated
when were you in India?
i lived there fifteen years as a foreign student
and after the big debacle (he pronounced it debackel I guess he meant
the crucifiction)
i retired to Kashmir
i didn't die I had
just passed out from the heat and stress
oh my god I said
what would be your teaching now
now you see the mess we've made of everything?
don't judge, meditate, understand that love is god celebrate
what your man Osho says
you are not your fucking ego.
Amen to that! I said

# Time and Transformation

This poor urban sapling
was abused by louts and pollarded by experts
ignored by most of us

now his roots reach deep
into the quiet dark earth of
time and transformation

his green crest rises in the evening sky
his branches dance in wind and rain
his flowers release a fragrance to our pillaged world

# We Listen to the Master

A swarm of bees
is twenty thousand
pixels nature's
glittering multiple
orgasm
we are set apart
in time and space
on a monitor you soon
refresh our plasma passion
smiles grow bright
fruitful as a buddha's
beguiling youthfulness

a colony divides to double up
clusters high overhead in an ash tree
bee scouts fly out
come back to dance
the immanence of
a true home
portions of our own dear selves
detach themselves till what was solid
eye and breast and chest
ravels apart in knitted webs of colour
flies home becomes the conscious
absence of ourselves

diffusion
is love's fusion

# Moving

spring springing
birds singing
sky hazing
blooms blooming
flies flying
cars passing
phone ringing
thoughts flitting
breath flowing
wheat waving
breath breathing
heart beating
day dying
eyes drowsing
life passing
death waiting
night falling
    who
who – unmoving –
watches moving

# Remember

beloved one
unknown or known
tonight remember
when you close your eyes
the radiance they are is lost to us
nor will you see
the bright starred smile
that glistens in the stars

beloved one
today remember
when you close your eye
and drift across
the boundless inland sea
the truth of you and all of us
unknown or known
is radiant in every grain of salt

## Credit card companies cut their limited appeal

The reason why cardholders with excellent credit histories are seeing their limits cut is obvious (No credit where it's due, Money, 13 March). Cardholders who religiously pay off the bill each month don't make any money (in terms of late interest payments) for the card companies: they don't want you. Credit card companies are in the business of making money (and right now they're desperate, especially if they're owned by a bank). Go and find another card, it's fairly easy. Companies don't seem to care about existing customers: they're hell bent on new customers.
**Allan Gould, Settle, North Yorkshire**

My card company cut my limit, without warning, to below what I owed, then charged me £12 for being over new limit, though I did get a ...
**smollett, guardian.co.uk/...**

I thought I was the only ... my limit was reduced ... £500 by Nationwide ... letter advising me of ... to a helpline for peop... found offensive as I ... debt, and always pa... promptly and in full ...
**magicali, guardian...**

The lender is ju... want to give yo... any more. It's ... so (it might no... Neither is it p... a good idea t... a debtor, no... pay for stuf... The bank is do... not doing it one... earned money ... some people ...
**oomph, guardi...**

Why is this ... a good credit rat... handle your finan... £15,000 limit. If yo... have maxed out ca... unsustainable mortg...
**halo572, guardian.co...**

Here's a tip: have the mone... bank before you spend it.
**Adam Hayward,**
**guardian.co.uk/money**

You always get those smug, patronising gits who bang on about putting money in the bank, and that they wouldn't be so feeble-minded as to have a credit card. Well try travelling around the world for work, hiring cars, booking into hotels, entertaining etc.
If you are human and can't file your expenses quickly enough, balances can rocket. In Paris a few weeks ago I tried to pay for a meal with my card. I knew to the pound what was on there. But the limit had been reduced without notice (apart from a letter I would collect on my return). It made me look a right mug as I scrambled for my debit card.

tailers. At some - dubbed "earn only" - you can't use reward money to reduce the cost of what you are buying and your balance will not appear on the card machine or till receipt.
Here are some of the current deals:

Until 15 May, spend £30 or more at Pizza Express and get £5 reward money ... all, between 1 April and 15 May, ... times with at least £25 of ... of the value of your ...

... Yo! Sushi ... of the bill ... to mpower ... direct and earning ... offer ends 12 ... won't ... on ... this being ... their spoilt bri... that we like and ...
**ozzydave, guar...co.uk/money**

Here in the New Fore... ... without an age... ...nts' hidden hefty charges... 13 March). I am a single moth... agricultural salary. It is a nigh... unable to afford to buy, and... trash by landlords and ag...
There has to be gov... ...ntion to assist...

...agency ...owners rent direct - which ...them the guarantees they want - and offers reliable tenants like me some security. Moving has really affected my kids. I have paid some £80,000 in rent in the last nine years as to buy on my salary was impossible.
Now I have to move again after a long tenancy. Goodbye deposit - landlords don't accept wear and tear. No houses to rent in the bus area for my kids' schools; I am at work long hours; have to borrow £2,000 to move, etc. I feel absolutely desperate.
**maylbuye, guardian.co.uk/money**

I have a property which I let. I never use letting agents because I object to giving 15%-20% of my rental income for something I can do almost for free.

ting agreements, available online or in library books. Credit checks are a relatively small fee compared with the potential loss of unpaid rent. I never charge tenants a fee because the credit check is for my benefit, and it's unjustifiable for agents to charge a tenant for this.
I mention in the adverts that I am not a letting agent and will not charge tenants a fee. I can't stand letting agents. They find my ad online and contact me, offering to let my property, even though the ad always specifies no contact from agents. They are leeches, taking money from tenant and landlord for doing virtually nothing. As a profession it is inadequately regulated, with no requirement for any qualifications whatsoever. Anyone can set themselves up as an estate/letting agent. As long as landlords and tenants persist in using them, we are all throwing money down the drain.
**chunderboss, guardian.co.uk/money**

## Quote was Direct Line to losing my custom

I've just had my home insurance renewal quote from Direct Line, which has followed a pattern for several ...rs, in being ridiculously increased ...ch undercut by its own website. (Current year £298; quoted renewal ...6) Direct Line's website £264).
... the past three years, when ... ed, Direct Line has agreed to ... ...t or near the online quote. ... year, though a discount was ... ...ingly offered, the premium still ... ...ly more than 50%.
... ...nutes on the web produced ...tter quotes for matching ...ed cover, so Direct Line has ... ...iness. Apparently customer ... ...n as not merely valueless ... ...nce for opportunist profit.
... ...t for every person like me. ... ...re will be many more who don't ... ...ew or challenge their automatic ...enewal. Loyalty isn't appreciated and, ...rhaps naively, I find that very sad.
**Ian Helm, Oldham**

## Taxed by interest rate conundrum of Isas

Your recent articles on Isas have been very interesting but they all raise the question of why banks pay lower rates of interest these than on other savings accounts. You would think Isas would be cheaper to run than other accounts since the banks don't have to go to the trouble of deducting income tax and paying it to HMRC. Surely the banks couldn't be nicking some of our tax relief, could they? I doubt it was the government's intention when creating Isas that banks should cream off half the customers' benefits.
**Martin Parker, Bookham, Surrey**

Write to Your Shout, Guardian Money.

# a with a Cream of
# n Sauce

After pasta with a cream of mushroom sauce
I sit not thinking much of anything
Puja reads aloud old Jung's idea that life
is like the unseen rhizome of a plant
we see the small shoots rise each year
the spread of foliage and flowers and fruit and seeds
that fold back into humus and decay

the root abides - vital and unseen
my memory wanders to this afternoon
inside the plastic tunnel I spent hours
mixing earth and kitchen-compost sand
and leaf-mould with a touch of wood-ash to deter the slugs
this mixture is my votive to the seeds
rain was hammering the roof and walls

reminding me of living in a bamboo hut in india
I went to be with a master went to learn the art
of being conscious and alert
present to the here and now
so that one day i could sit digesting
pasta with a cream of mushroom sauce
happily abiding in the present

TWO EYES CLOSED
ONE EYE
OPEN

# Arising Song

arising song
from wren and thrush
– dawn chorus –
takes its place
in luminous
unfettered self

poets gift wrap
skilful lines
alliterated rhymes
in songs without
small print
or an end

the bird
and poet
both are fettered

where they sing from
is their real home
self itself

# Gravity and Grace

Gravity is lord
right now he holds
this body (refined fauna) to the bed
the bed to the floor
to the poor dead earth cold
rain is pulled down to
steep the trees that are
the wood that makes the moulded
bed

Meanwhile grace raises trees
and birdsong human spirits
and at dawn the pulsing
rushing sun
she is high queen she is mother
of all that rises
her human subjects
accept in her the one
wonder

# All Around

(Heaven and Hell)

I don't know!
the whole thing's
a bitch
she loves me
she stands me up
there's no cessation
to the whole assembled
waves of pain
the mind
a boiling kettle
this is not something
i can easily clear
neither the hand-off
nor the looming
skeleton his scythe
poised already
oh no
hell is exactly
this

i suspect though
when the witness
is evoked
it is seen
that the place
for all this drama
sound and fury
is a wide stage
of infinite peace and silence
inside the heart
inside each moment
inside the very
roar and clatter
the mind
can't grasp it
heaven
exactly is
this stillness
all around

# No Boundaries
for you my daughters
Arabella Beatrice Melita

The recently invented
universe
(fourteen billion years with Mr Einstein's recent marriage to the
quantum guys)
revolves around
itself
now here's the thing
you are
the universe
in microcosm
each humming molecule
dancing to the
measure of
unsayable immensity
you are the centre
and periphery
you call the tune
you are the tune
no boundaries
(despite what I keep saying about laying firm your lines of demarcation)
so why not dance
the wild expansion
of the galaxies
the radiance of supernova
the delicate delight of
shy red dwarfs
riding through our
brilliant blood
let's dance

# I Blame the Lodger

I blame the lodger
up there in his
sad stuffy loft
i got stung not
once but twenty
times a right peppering
the grass needs
cutting he says
lettuce seeds to be sown
peas transplanted
etcetera etcetera
don't postpone
get on with it
the warning signs
were there
looming plum-dark
thunder clouds
it's the mid-season
zone of scarcity
the hives have
everything to lose
bees now are
naturally defensive
they don't like
the high pitch
of the strimmer
the air was close
I listened to the
sad tyrannical
mind
caused grace
to suffer dead bees
and a painful face

# Water Lily

A water lily
on the black enamel
level of the pond
over-lapping
layers of purple petals
star-like round
the core gold
crown of filaments
scissile inner circles
overhang
the hollow centre

look
look at this obscurity
this vacancy

the purple petals
and the gold corona
quiver on the edge of
detonation
the lily's stem
descends to roots
in dark prenatal slime

we are this lily
says the master
the vacancy
the tender beauty
the awaiting
the gold
the mud
we are this lily

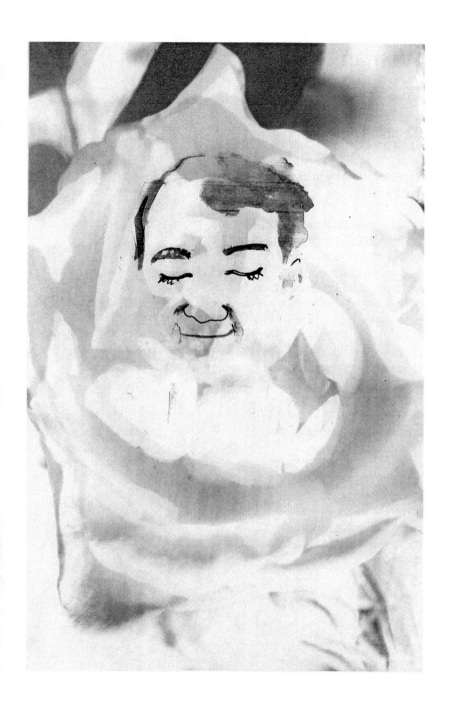

# Woman

All we ever wanted
I tell you
was to melt into the woman
sex is an effort
to reach into
a greater meeting with
infinity

I gaze at you matisse models
fashion catalogues film clips
let slip my boundaries in their raven
hair your half-closed eyes
and thoughtful smile the haven
of their placid silken
moorings

I have grown slowly
to understand there's no out there
out there
the fusion with existence
with you
is here in this protesting
particularity

now we lie quiet together
intimate and alone please
allow me to adore you
write this private unpoetic
metaphor out of
the story
thus

# Well Versed Master

lost
on the crooked highway
to my death
in school and then in acts of war
in dreaming spires and schools of thought
in broken-hearted love affairs
and brilliant flawed marriages
I exhale a cloud of craving
for you

you
called me four thousand eight hundred
and seventy five miles
to grow your coriander and green beans
to fly lop-winged
over the dark forgotten sky
burn fake tomorrows and cancelled yesterdays
drink soft rain in the
desert

you
beloved well-versed master
take from me
what I do not have
dawn and day and dusk
you give me what I already am
a sky with no horizon
a life that lives
itself

# What is Meditation?

Ask an artist
      what is meditation
She will say
      the white enticement of a canvas
Ask a singer
      what is meditation
He will say
      the silence in the roaring storm
Ask a poet
      paper without words
Ask a dancer
      The whirl of neutrons and electrons
Ask anyone you meet
      what is meditation
      low sunlight on the leaves at dawn
      spontaneity of kids
      water surging from a spring
      singing to a million willing faces
      the occasion of an orgasm

Ask enlightened ones
      what is meditation
They scratch their head
      and smile into their cappuccino.

# Good Day Mr Death

*This morning these lines came to me:*

Rush hour
and I watch the queue
inch forward
till I see the ticket hatch
where death issues you
your warrant

I believe
death is a fiction
someone else's verdict
on your body's health
not on the real you
not the real you
who's afraid of death I ask myself
I am a gardener after all

*Later in the morning the telephone rang*
*Jocelyn had died*

Immediately
my hard achieved tranquillity
poured out through the eyes
she loved me
gave me useful words and home baked cakes
I am swept out to sea

Perhaps it's best to greet death
with no big ideas
no big beliefs
a bald not knowing
and a cordial - Good day Mr Death

# Haiku

After meditation
the big tree outside
crowds into my room


Rainbow Lorikeets
and the scent of gardenias
we still mess the world up


The dark night sky,
rain on dead leaves;
already too many words


A white Cockatoo
plumps into the dark tree
so I write this


In this suburban street
are Mynah birds millionaires
and a thin crescent moon

# When I Say You're Beautiful

When i say you're beautiful
I'm not just speaking in the idiom of mirrors
I'm speaking of your unseen core
formed of fire and ice and centuries of mountain rivulets

I'm speaking of the seasons of your being –
spring time's scented buds that draw the bees
the petals that shower radiance
your fruitfulness your graceful yield to winter silence

The beauty that I greet in you is candle flames
in currents of dim air a falcon floating on a thermal
the different sameness of the dawn
rising to revere our worried world

I'm speaking of what's seen with inner eyes
of what will slip the handcuffs of the best poetic words
I'm speaking both the language of the mirrors
and the silence of the heart to say – you're beautiful

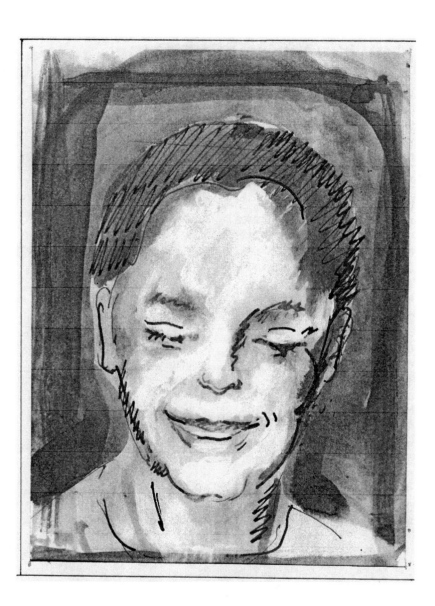

# Now it's Different

the old home
musty clustered full of
porcelain do's and dont's
was a bane for sleeping
real life was outside

i was van gogh trudging
the plain of arles with
easel oil-paints brushes canvases
to wrestle chrome green strokes
a wash of crimson lake against the umber
counterpoint of factory chimneys
a beggar swopping crusts
and home brew in cracked
plastic bottles

one kaleidoscopic day
on the sea shore
a white robed ocean giant
rose above the streaming foam
look! look in!
flush out your rooms
without a within there is no true without

today one wall is sunrise
the roof a cornflower sky
the universe a virgin canvas
there's so much room at home

Lightning Source UK Ltd.
Milton Keynes UK
UKOW03f0629100814

236655UK00001B/44/P